GOD DOES NOT WANT YOUR BILL MONEY

Dispelling the Tainted Doctrine
of Tithes and Offerings

The Truth Series Vol. 1

Desimber Rose Wattleton

God Does Not Want Your Bill Money
Dispelling the Tainted Doctrine of Tithes
and Offerings

Copyright © 2019 Desimber Rose Wattleton
All Rights Reserved

3-In-3 Publishing
P.O. Box 1075
Taylors, SC 29687
order@3in3Publishing.com

No part of this book may be reproduced or transmitted in any form or by any means electronic or mechanical, including recording, photocopying, or by any information storage and retrieval system without written permission from the publisher, referred to as Desimber Rose Wattleton.

Please direct your inquiries to the aforementioned address or submit by email to
order@3in3publishing.com

Unless otherwise noted, all scripture quotations are from the New King James Version of the Holy Bible, Copyright 1979, 1980, 1982 by Thomas Nelson, Inc. Used by permission. All rights reserved.

GOD DOES NOT WANT YOUR BILL MONEY

DEDICATION

This book is dedicated to The Body of Christ, and to all those who want to Know The Truth.

SPEAK ON IT

"I've learned all my life in church that you are supposed to tithe 10%. My question is what if after taking God's 10% off top; you are tremendously short of paying your bills? I know I'm supposed to put all my trust in him, but when doing my budget and budgeting in tithes of 10%, I'm coming up short for bills and household expenses. Spiritually I want to believe, but on paper the negative numbers are creating fear, worry, confusion and frustration."

- Udrieka Chapman

"Growing up in my dad's church I was taught that tithing was apart of the Mosaic law and that we are not under that law anymore so I didn't tithe. After my dad passed I joined a church that taught tithing but not biblically. Basically it was like, how did you think the bills get paid if you don't tithe? Later I joined a ministry that taught although tithing was a law, it's still a good principle and I tithed for 8 years with that perspective. Today. I am the pastor of a ministry and I will teach the word, be a cheerful giver and God gives seed to the sower. We are free through Christ to give as we have been blessed."

- Pastor Torey Hill, The Renewal House

"When I first became saved and began to think about tithing, I was thinking along the line of "I have bills to pay." I didn't see how only ten percent of my income would assist Him in anything He had to do, and I was hesitant. I never looked at it as stewardship, for truthfully the entire check was His because I was His! I was not taught that then. Eventually I overcame the struggle and began to tithe faithfully. I should not be concerned about bills, anyway, because He is the One taking care of me. I still hear people say that it is for the Old Testament only, or that it isn't money but should be fruit or

vegetables, etc. I walk according to the conviction in me, and I am led to tithe so that there is meat in the house, as it is stated in Malachi. To each his own, but as for me and mine, we are going to serve the Lord with my brother Joshua! The Body needs to be reminded that God Does Not Want Your Bill Money, but He does want His money!! The tithe belongs to the Lord."
- *Pastor Stephanie Johnson-Rice*
Chains Broken Deliverance Ministries

"I believe tithing is a wonderful principle of the kingdom if educated correctly and used appropriately. However, we know over time, tithe and offering has been misunderstood by the body of Christ and misused for personal gain by leaders in the body of Christ. I personally remember giving an offering of 3 cent, because just like the woman with the widow's mite…that's all I had. I had no gas in my car, when I went to church or returned home. I checked my mailbox and I had a check for 50.00. I believe tithing is a principle that is set by God for 2 reasons, 1 to take care of the things of this world such as the building, lights, etc, outreach, and more. Secondly, it increases our faith and trust in God that ultimately, he is our provider and if we take care of His priorities, he will take care of ours."
- *Brandy Hunt, Author*
Dealing with the Hand I was Dealt

"Well, I was never one to tithe but went to a church that offered a money back challenge. They said if you tithe up front and God doesn't bless you in some way, they will give your tithe back. We took a leap of faith and started tithing up front. Even though the twins had just been released from NICU, I had quit my job to take care of them and myself do health reasons and we were over $500,000 in medical debt. And God did bless us. He improved areas in our marriage,

we got better at living beneath or means. We took Dave Ramsey's financial peace university course and are now non-mortgage debt free, have a more solid marriage and a stronger faith as a family. The Bible calls us to tithe. God blesses us with our income and it is a lack of faith to believe that God won't provide for us if we give him back 10 percent. I believe not tithing is directly tied to a lack of faith and after taking the leap and experiencing God's Grace in our lives, I'll never not tithe again. God is faithful. God is good."
- *Mercedes Phillips*

"I don't have a problem with tithing. I do tithe when I go to church, my problem is consistency with going to church. Sometimes I tithe online when I don't go. I don't give a certain amount I just give."
- *Bambi Griggs*

"In the beginning I really didn't understand tithing at first. I just thought it was that the church just wanted my money so to speak and then I started to realize that we were supposed to bring our money into the storehouse, it was for the body of Christ, for the fellowship at the church. There was a period that I would not tithe and then I noticed that my finances would decrease, and when I got tired of it I'd start tithing and that's when the increase started so I'm a firm believer of tithing. Once upon a time I would have never gave anything to anyone so when I tithe now it's like I'm testing my faith."
- *Khadiya Sankoh-Henry*
The Underground Praize Mix Radio Show

"This is going to set some folks free!"
- *Nicholas Dyson*

GOD DOES NOT WANT YOUR BILL MONEY

"Tithing is Not A Bill, It is An Opportunity to BE Obedient to The True And Living GOD!!! THIS Book Will Encourage The Readers to Further Study The Biblical Principles of Tithing And Examine Our Lives And FRUIT Harvest as It Relates to Tithing or Not!!! Tithing is An Opportunity to SOW InTo The KingDom of GOD By Helping Meet the Needs of The CHURCH... The BElievers, The Building And The Under Shepherd of The House!!! Serve GOD!!! Serve Others!!! And God WILL Serve YOU!!!"

Reverend J. Senay Spurgeon
J. Senay Spurgeon Ministries, Inc.
Queendom Affirmation Apparel Line

GOD DOES NOT WANT YOUR BILL MONEY

Table of Contents

DEDICATION iii

SPEAK ON IT iv

FOREWORD 11

INTRODUCTION 13

CHAPTER 1 in the beginning 16

CHAPTER 2 the prosperity lie 25

CHAPTER 3 giving is worship 41

CHAPTER 4 not by sight 51

CHAPTER 5 giving from vs. giving to 58

Scriptural References 67

A Note from the Author 70

FOREWORD

Fore·word
/ˈfôrˌwərd/

noun
a short introduction to a book, typically by a person other than the author.

I thought about asking someone to write a Foreword for this book, but then I realized the Word was forewritten…

"Remember this: Whoever sows sparingly will also reap sparingly, and whoever sows generously will also reap generously. Each of you should give what you have decided in your heart to give, not reluctantly or under compulsion, for God loves a cheerful giver.

And God is able to bless you abundantly, so that in all things at all times, having all that you need, you will abound in every good work. As it is written: "They have freely scattered their gifts to the poor; their righteousness endures forever.

Now he who supplies seed to the sower and bread for food will also supply and increase your store of seed and will enlarge the harvest of your righteousness. You will be enriched in every way so that you can be generous on every occasion, and through us your generosity will result in thanksgiving to God.

This service that you perform is not only supplying the needs of the Lord's people but is also overflowing in many expressions of thanks to God. Because of the service by which you have proved yourselves, others will praise God for the obedience that accompanies your confession of the gospel of Christ, and for your generosity in sharing with them and with everyone else.

And in their prayers for you their hearts will go out to you, because of the surpassing grace God has given you. Thanks be to God for His indescribable gift!"

2 Corinthians 9:6-14 (NIV)
Author, The Apostle Paul

INTRODUCTION

Tithing is biblical. Now that we've established that fact, we can focus on the objective of this book, which is to expose the tainted teaching of tithes and offerings as a mandate or commandment from God, which is a false doctrine that simply cannot prevail when held up to the light of the Gospel.

It has been the practice of The Church in general to conflate and confuse commandments with principles. For example, you will not find a commandment from God in the Bible that states, "Thou shalt not drink." But you will find a principle concerning the consumption of alcohol in Proverbs 23:20-21 which states, "Do not mix with winebibbers (drunks), Or with gluttonous eaters of meat; For the drunkard and the glutton will come to poverty, and drowsiness will clothe a man with rags." (NKJV) Even though the Scriptures clearly state here and in the New Testament not to engage in drunkenness or associate with those that do, many in the church have misinterpreted the Scriptures and taught that drinking any alcohol whatsoever is a sin.

There are many more examples I could give, but the bottom line is we have to study this Word for ourselves, and see what God has to say about matters concerning our daily living and application of His Word. God does not expect us to live up to the expectations of others or be held accountable to the convictions of others. And yet, there are so many preachers and pastors who continue to preach their own convictions as commandments.

It is imperative that we understand the concept of giving and stewardship as believers. I believe God would have his children to know the Truth, not the truth as seen through the taint of tradition, religion, and individual conviction, but *His* truth, *His* Gospel, and *His* Word, which requires no additions or subtractions.

Satan knows that agreement is one of the most powerful principles a Christian can uphold. If he can get you to agree with a faithless interpretation of the Gospel that would have you to believe your blessings are based on how much money you give to the church, then he has convinced you to disagree with the Gospel, and the sufficient sacrifice of Christ, when Jesus said on the cross, "It is finished." If he can convince you that you owe God something and come into agreement with others that it is possible to rob God when it comes to money, then he has successfully made grace of no effect in your life.

My prayer is that everyone who reads this book receives an understanding of the Principle of Tithing, and the expectations of God Himself, compared to what has been taught and handed down through the years in the Body of Christ.

Most importantly, it is my heart's desire that the

believers walk victoriously in their faith, free from the bondage of guilt and condemnation in every area of their lives, that they may receive the fullness of Grace, the depth of God's mercy, and the complete expanse of salvation through Christ Jesus.

CHAPTER 1
in the beginning

"If you destroy the foundations of anything, the structure will collapse. If you want to destroy any building, you are guaranteed early success if you destroy the foundations."
-Ken Ham

There is not anything still standing, whenever it was built, that was not built on some kind of foundation. As believers, we have in our possession The Bible, which we believe is the infallible truth, written by man, but inspired by God Himself. It is the foundation for everything we do, including our giving, which is why the enemy has fought so hard to put distance between us and the Gospel of Grace through rules, rituals, and regulations.

This is why it is so important that the false foundation and tainted doctrine of mandatory tithing be torn down, that we may be built up in our faith upon the firm foundation of knowledge and understanding. In order to dispel the myth, we must begin at the beginning, where the principle of tithing originated, in order to understand why we are neither obligated nor accountable to mandatory tithing. This practice originates in the Pentateuch, which is the first five books of the Bible, Genesis through Deuteronomy. These five books contain the Mosaic Law and instructions concerning how these laws were to be observed and enforced. These laws were given to Moses by God for the children of Israel, and represent the first covenant of righteousness and standard of living issued by God, directly to the children of Israel.

The first time the word tithe is used in the Bible is in Genesis 14:20. Abram, later known as Abraham, pursued and defeated King Chedorlaomar with only 318 men after finding out his nephew Lot had been captured. Knowing it could only have been the hand of God interceding for him, and thus ensuring his victory, he gave a tithe to Melchizedek, a priest and king of Salem (Read Genesis Chapter 14 for the complete account of these events).

This tithe was completely voluntary and may have been from all of Abram's spoils or the best of Abram's spoils, the scripture is not specific in this aspect. What we do know is that Abram was inspired or motivated to offer this tithe because of the victory, not for the victory. In other words, Abram didn't tithe **FOR** a blessing, he tithed **FROM** a blessing. This was solely an act of gratitude by Abram, not a fulfillment of obligation.

The first mention of giving to God from one's substance as a mandate is found in Exodus 22:29-30, which states, "You shall not delay to offer the first of your ripe produce and your juices. The firstborn of your sons you shall give to Me. Likewise you shall do with your oxen and your sheep, it shall be with its mother seven days; on the eighth day you shall give it to Me."

We can interpret this both literally and spiritually. The offering of produce, juices, and animals was literal. The offering of first-born sons was spiritual; these were dedicated to God in covenant and service, to become the priests of their households, to uphold the law and life of reverence to God. The scriptures go on to reveal three types of tithing implemented as part of the Mosaic Law.

First, there were tithes for the support of the Levites, those who have been chosen by God specifically for tabernacle service. Their lives were completely dedicated to the function and service as priests of the tabernacle. This was their source of income, what could be considered compensation for that service as they had no other inheritance or duty but to work in the House of God. You will find this in Numbers, Chapter 18:21-24.

21 And, behold, I have given the children of Levi all the tenth in Israel for an inheritance, for their service which they serve, even the service of the tabernacle of the congregation.

22 Neither must the children of Israel henceforth come nigh the tabernacle of the congregation, lest they bear sin, and die.

23 But the Levites shall do the service of the tabernacle of the congregation, and they shall bear their iniquity: it shall be a statute forever throughout your generations, that among the children of Israel they have no inheritance.

24 But the tithes of the children of Israel, which they offer as an heave offering unto the Lord, I have given to the Levites to inherit: therefore I have said unto them, Among the children of Israel they shall have no inheritance.

You see here that God appointed the Levites to life-long service in the tabernacle, which meant they had no inheritance among the Children of Israel, no alternative employment, and no other source of provision or wealth. The tithe was intended to be their provision and ultimately the inheritance that sustained them as they carried out their calling to the service of the tabernacle and God's people. If you read Numbers

18:25-29, you will see that the Levites were also required to give a tithe from the tithes and offerings they received.

Second, there were tithes and offerings given for the annual convocations or formal assemblies, which were accompanied by celebrations and festivals. This tithe was to be brought to the annual festival and consumed in fellowship and in the presence of God. This was not to substitute the Levitical tithe but was to be brought in addition to it. You will find this in Deuteronomy 14:22-27:

22 Be sure to set aside a tenth of all that your fields produce each year. 23 Eat the tithe of your grain, new wine and olive oil, and the firstborn of your herds and flocks in the presence of the Lord your God at the place he will choose as a dwelling for his Name, so that you may learn to revere the Lord your God always.

24 But if that place is too distant and you have been blessed by the Lord your God and cannot carry your tithe (because the place where the Lord will choose to put his Name is so far away),

25 then exchange your tithe for silver, and take the silver with you and go to the place the Lord your God will choose.

26 Use the silver to buy whatever you like: cattle, sheep, wine or other fermented drink, or anything you wish. Then you and your household shall eat there in the presence of the Lord your God and rejoice.

27 And do not neglect the Levites living in your towns, for they have no allotment or inheritance of their own.

Third, there were tithes offered every three years for benevolence, or charity. This was also a tithe of produce and was stored up within the cities of the land for the care of Levitical priests and those in need. This is also found in Deuteronomy 14:28-29:

28 At the end of three years thou shalt bring forth all the tithe of thine increase the same year, and shalt lay it up within thy gates:

29 And the Levite, (because he hath no part nor inheritance with thee,) and the stranger, and the fatherless, and the widow, which are within thy gates, shall come, and shall eat and be satisfied; that the Lord thy God may bless thee in all the work of thine hand which thou doest.

If you add all of this up, it comes to much more than 10% of one's finances. However, most times no other portion of scripture except the financial aspect of tithing is taught. No matter how it's been taught, we can plainly see that tithing is biblical. The Bible says in 2 Timothy 3:16 that *"All scripture is given by inspiration of God, and is profitable for doctrine, for reproof, for correction, for instruction in righteousness."* So, we know that we should take notice of this if it is mentioned in the Bible, because there is certainly not one word wasted, or one scripture that cannot be applied to our lives in some way today.

The laws and practices we have read were given directly to the Israelites from God. And the primary function of the tithes was to maintain the Levitical Priests and the Temple. We may have many different interpretations of Scripture, but one thing we should be able to agree upon is the fact that not a single person reading this book is appointed to the Levitical Priesthood, nor are any of us, not even full-time pastors, completely devoted to temple service. Even if you are pastoring full-time, you still have an inheritance, you still have homes, land, and even businesses that you likely intend to pass on to your children.

Furthermore, the Scriptures state that Jesus Christ is now our Eternal Priest, who, through his sacrifice has replaced the order of the Levitical Priesthood with an eternal Priesthood – Hebrews 7:11-14

11 Therefore, if perfection were through the Levitical priesthood (for under it the people received the law), what further need was there that another priest should rise according to the order of Melchizedek, and not be called according to the order of Aaron? 12 For the priesthood being changed, of necessity there is also a change of the law. 13 For He of whom these things are spoken belongs to another tribe, from which no man has officiated at the altar.

14 For it is evident that our Lord arose from Judah, of which tribe Moses spoke nothing concerning priesthood. 15 And it is yet far more evident if, in the likeness of Melchizedek, there arises another priest 16 who has come, not according to the law of a fleshly commandment, but according to the power of an endless life. 17 For He testifies: "You are a priest forever According to the order of Melchizedek."

Although we no longer have need for an earthly priesthood to make intercession and sacrifices for us, we do, and always will, have among us the poor, the widow, and the orphan. And for this reason and others, the tithes and offerings go a long way to aid the missions of the church, to expand the reach of the church into the local community and throughout the world, to provide a means to fulfil the commission of Christ.

But it's how we choose to apply the Word of God that determines whether that Word becomes a blessing or a burden. Even in the day the law was written, it was not intended by God to be a burden on His people, but intended to establish a standard for righteous living, civil interaction, and maintain the work of the ministry. Clearly, tithing is biblical, and the Word of God should be the foundation for everything we do, but with pastors blatantly asking their congregations to buy them private jets, and using the people's money to live extravagant lifestyles, it is no wonder many have become disaffected by preachers and disillusioned by the concept of tithes and offerings to the church.

Even believers can become discouraged, that's why it's not enough for us to read the Bible, study the letter of the law, or even know what the scriptures say. What benefit is it to the Body of Christ if we can quote the scriptures word for word but fail to understand the intent of the Author? It is the Holy Spirit that leads and guides us into all truth (John 16:13), and we have an obligation to not only study God's Word, but seek His intent, to reconcile our knowledge with grace, and to apply it accordingly.

CHAPTER 2
the prosperity lie

"The most intangible, and therefore the worst kind of a lie, is a half-truth. This is the peculiar device of a conscientious detractor." -Washington Allston

You've seen it, we've all seen it, a prayer line, a traveling prophet or prophetess, a late-night televangelist, claiming that if you just sow a three hundred dollar seed, a thousand dollar seed, or I've even seen them say a forty-four dollar seed, somehow the windows of heaven are going to open up and pour you out a blessing you won't have room to receive. On any given Sunday, you can step into a church and find someone chiding God's people about giving, you can turn on the television or go online and find a "prosperity preacher". And it's actually really sad, because every preacher should be a prosperity preacher, since it's God Himself who wants us to prosper (3 John 1:2). But now that term has a negative connotation and has come to be associated with preachers who specifically and primarily associate the blessings of God, wealth, and material possessions with tithes and offerings.

We have established that tithing is biblical, there is no question about that. But it is how the Word of God is used that is often the cause of so much confusion, misinterpretations, and unfortunately, deliberate misrepresentation, which have for years created a stumbling block where there should be a stepping stone.

One of those stumbling blocks is manipulation. Sometimes it is deliberate, and other times it is a result of ignorance, not knowing what the truth is, not being taught the biblical history of tithing, or not taking the initiative to search the scriptures and ask God for understanding, as we have been instructed to do in James 1:5, *"If any of you lacks wisdom, let him ask of God, who gives to all liberally and without reproach, and it will be given to him."*

Over the years I've been to many churches and I've seen tithes and offerings handled many different ways. There's the auction style offering where people are asked to stand or come forward if they have a certain amount of money, which can make those who don't have that amount feel inferior to those who do. There's what I like to call the re-run offering, where people come around to give and while they are giving there are deacons counting the money right there, and if they have not reached their goal, they continue to ask the people to come until they reach the financial goal, which is usually unknown and not announced to the congregation. Then there's the fire and brimstone offering, where the pastor or deacon basically reprimands the people before they even have a chance to give! Telling, or yelling at them, saying they will be cursed if they don't tithe, and that all types of hell will break loose in their lives, that basically their whole life will begin to fall apart if they should dare rob God of the tithe.

The problem with each of these is that there is a sliver of truth in each one of them, but manipulation and condemnation overshadow the blessing of giving. It is true, that if there is a certain amount God is leading you to give you should be obedient. It is true, that if there is a need in the ministry, according to God's will, the people should give to meet the need as lead by the Holy Spirit. And yes, it is also true, that if we are disobedient to the voice of God there can sometimes be adverse consequences. However, there is no biblical foundation for using guilt as a tool to prompt people to give. As a matter of fact, Romans

8:1 says, *"there is therefore now no condemnation to those who are in Christ Jesus, who do not walk according to the flesh, but according to the Spirit."* So, when guilt is used as a means to prompt the believer to do something God has asked him or her to do, this is manipulation, it can even be considered a form of witchcraft.

We have to ask ourselves, why would God use guilt and condemnation as a means to encourage us to give? The answer is He would not, and does not. Yet, many will use scripture as a means of manipulating people to give out of guilt, rather than their giving being a direct response to the Holy Spirit, a result of their growth in the Word of God, their desire to see the objectives of the ministry met, and their ability to sow into the advancement of a kingdom agenda, which are the ONLY reasons anyone should be giving. If we are giving for any other reasons, this is what the scriptures call compulsion in 2 Corinthians 9:7, which says *"Each one should give what he has decided in his heart to give, not out of regret or compulsion."* I like the way the New Living Translation (NLT) puts it, *"You must each decide in your heart how much to give. And don't give reluctantly or in response to pressure. "For God loves a person who gives cheerfully."*

Pick 8 out of any 10 churches and you will likely hear a certain scripture used... Every Single Sunday... at offering time, and that is Malachi 3:8-10, which says:

"'Will a man rob God? Yet you have robbed Me! But you say, In what way have we robbed You? In tithes and offerings. You are cursed with a curse, for you have robbed Me, even this whole nation. Bring all the tithes into the storehouse, that there may be food in My house, And try Me now in this.' Says the Lord of hosts, If I will not open for you the windows of heaven and pour out for you such blessing that there will not be room enough to receive it."

You may have heard this scripture or multiple variations of it. However, the fact about this book and these scriptures that cannot be ignored is that it was written by the Prophet Malachi concerning the sinful state of the Israelites; which we have learned are the ones who received the Mosaic Law. They had once again strayed away from God and the law. There were dishonorable offerings being given, corrupt priests causing people to stumble, infidelity with foreign women. In addition to this, they were not giving the tithes as commanded, which meant the Levites could not focus on their duties to the temple and had to find other ways to provide for themselves, the yearly convocation and festivals became difficult or were not held at all and the needs of the poor were not being adequately met.

There is a significant point to be made here. God has specifically instructed us not to give under pressure. However, when people don't give, the ministry suffers. The pastor or shepherd cannot focus solely on building the ministry if he or she must constantly be concerned with keeping the lights and water on at the church, paying the lease or mortgage on the building, or keeping outreach programs staffed and supplied. It would be very difficult to have successful meetings or conferences that require a significant amount of finances. And charitable works in the church or local community will suffer for lack of funding. So, while we should not be giving under pressure, we should have our ear and heart open to the voice of God concerning our giving.

There is no question that finances are a very important part of ministry, and without finances the ministry is stifled. Therefore, the portion of scripture that says God is robbed and even the whole nation is robbed is true in that when people refrain from giving, the kingdom agenda is hindered, which can in fact have a global impact. But context matters, and it's important that we establish the context for these Scriptures to see how they should be applied today.

The Book of Malachi was written to the Israelites as a rebuke and a warning in response to their backslidden state concerning their observance of the law and ungodly social behavior. But what is most important about this book, but hardly ever… if ever… preached in church, is that the book was more of a rebuke of the priests than the people. Pastors like to zero in on Malachi 3:10 but completely ignore that the harshest rebuke was of the priests, you see this in Malachi 1:6-8 –

> *"A son honors his father, And a servant his master. If then I am the Father, Where is My honor? And if I am a Master, Where is My reverence? Says the Lord of hosts To you priests who despise My name. Yet you say, 'In what way have we despised Your name?'*
>
> *7 "You offer defiled food on My altar, But say, 'In what way have we defiled You?' By saying, 'The table of the Lord is contemptible.' 8 And when you offer the blind as a sacrifice, Is it not evil? And when you offer the lame and sick, Is it not evil? Offer it then to your governor! Would he be pleased with you? Would he accept you favorably? Says the Lord of hosts."*

Not only is the Book of Malachi a rebuke of the priests, but a prophecy concerning the spread of the Gospel and gift of salvation to the Gentiles, which we find in Malachi 1:11 –

> *"For from the rising of the sun, even to its going down, My name shall be great among the Gentiles; In every place incense shall be offered to My name, And a pure offering; For My name shall be great among the nations," Says the Lord of hosts."*

Isn't it amazing that all in one book, God is rebuking the priests, warning the people, and speaking forward to a time when faith and grace will replace the Law of Moses? I have a question for the preachers, pastors, and spiritual leaders preaching tithes as a commandment and obligation to God's children. Do you trust God? Are you seeking Him? Have you searched the Scriptures for yourself concerning the matter? When is the last time you read the entire Book of Malachi? Did you see where the Bible makes it clear in Malachi 2:1-2 that this message is for the Priests?

> *"And now, O priests, this commandment is for you. 2 If you will not hear, And if you will not take it to heart, To give glory to My name," Says the Lord of hosts, "I will send a curse upon you, And I will curse your blessings. Yes, I have cursed them already, Because you do not take it to heart."*

Did you see where it was the priests who were not ministering to the people with pure knowledge, bringing *"the stolen, the lame, and the sick"* offerings to God (Malachi 1:13), and through their actions causing the Israelites to take an irreverent position toward God and the Law? – Malachi 2:7-9

> *"For the lips of a priest should keep knowledge, And people should seek the law from his mouth; For he is the messenger of the Lord of hosts. 8 But*

you have departed from the way; You have caused many to stumble at the law. You have corrupted the covenant of Levi," Says the Lord of hosts. 9 "Therefore I also have made you contemptible and base Before all the people, Because you have not kept My ways But have shown partiality in the law."

Did you see where Malachi called out those who would be judged including those who were Exploiting the working class, the vulnerable, and turning away the immigrants? – Malachi 3:5

And I will come near you for judgment; I will be a swift witness Against sorcerers, Against adulterers, Against perjurers, Against those who exploit wage earners and widows and orphans, And against those who turn away an alien — Because they do not fear Me," Says the Lord of hosts.

ALL of this comes before you even get to Malachi 3:10, have you seen it? Or have you chosen to ignore it? Because if we as spiritual leaders read this with an open heart and ear to the Spirit of the Living God, we must come to the conclusion that the mandate is not on the congregation but on US! If we are preaching the Gospel to God's people with Pure Knowledge, if we are upholding a standard of righteous living in our Own Lives, if we have truly set our hands to the plough to diligently engage in the work of the

Kingdom, if we take our call seriously, then we will not have to beat up God's people with the Word to get them to give, and we would fear God enough not to exploit them. The more I listen to preachers speak about tithes the more it sounds like words without knowledge, an age-old repetition of a faithless call to action that God never required of born again believers.

As leaders we are called to preach the Gospel, not our personal convictions. The Gospel of Grace does not require the Gentiles to tithe, this is a fact. There is No Commandment to the New Testament Church, to those who have received Christ as Savior to tithe. And the few times Jesus did mention it, he was mentioning it in the midst of a rebuke and as an example of self-righteousness to who? The Sadducees and Pharisees… again, another rebuke of spiritual leaders, Not the people.

Tithing, when practiced for the right reasons, is an awesome principle to abide by, not because of religion, but because of relationship with God. But we cannot treat commandments and principles the same, they are not the same. Not keeping commandments can separate us from God, not abiding by principles or living a principled life, can keep us from living victoriously and hinders our ability to be an effective witness for God.

How can we know the difference between a commandment and a principle? The best thing you can do is study the Word, which God has called upon each of us to do for ourselves in 2 Timothy 2:15. If we look to God's Word and ask for understanding, the Holy Spirit will reveal not only the Word of God, but His intent. (See John 16:13-15).

Commandments are the moral framework God has given us for righteous living, and disobeying them causes us to walk in sin, which separates us from God. Principles are wisdom for practical life application and are intended to help us walk circumspectly in the world as good representatives of the Gospel; and to position us to experience an abundant life of health and wealth through good stewardship of our bodies, time, talent, and resources. For example, according to the Mosaic Law, if one had committed fornication, the judgment would be carried out by that individual being stoned to death. Since Jesus fulfilled the law with grace and forgiveness, then we are able to repent and ask God's forgiveness. The Bible says the wages of sin is death, so we will indeed die, but we will not be stoned to death as a penalty for our actions, and we won't be dead eternally but will inherit eternal life, which is the gift of forgiveness through salvation.

We must be careful not to enter into a state of self-righteousness by picking and choosing which parts of the Mosaic Law we will adhere to and which parts we won't. Once again, these laws were given to the

Israelites. Although the basic principles of morality are found in these laws, they also contain culturally specific tenets and instructions specific to the time they were written and the culture of the people to which they were given. That is why it is so important to study the scriptures for yourself, to see what God was saying then, how God spoke to the people then, how God differentiated His people then and how God speaks to His people and differentiates them from the world now.

You may ask yourself, if tithing is not mandatory, why do some preach that it is? There are various reasons for this, one of the primary reasons is ignorance, just not knowing the truth. Something has been preached for years, and those who heard it never went to the scriptures to confirm whether or not it was true, they just believed it without question and also taught others the same thing, who also believed it without question.

Then there are some who teach tithing as mandatory because they have ulterior motives; their hearts are not in the right place, they don't care about the sheep and they want to get anything the sheep will allow them to have. I actually believe these are the minority. The majority of those teaching that tithing is mandatory are dealing with a combination of ignorance and lack of faith. Why lack of faith? Because they have come up hearing that this is mandatory, this is what good Christians are supposed to do, this is what saved people have to do and so they are teaching it. In addition, God has called them, and chosen them for ministry, and given them a vision of what He is going to do in their lives and in the ministries He has made them stewards of, and when things start getting tough, when the vision God gave them doesn't seem to be manifesting quickly enough, when things don't look like they're going to work out how God told them it would, they become desperate and afraid.

What are they afraid of? They're afraid to fail, afraid of what people will think, afraid their image will be damaged, and they begin to pass that burden on to the sheep in the way of badgering them and guilting them into giving. You will know when this is happening; it is very obvious, and usually creates a negative emotional response. The pastor or leader will begin to speak more and more about giving than usual. There may be an offering raised at every meeting no matter how big or small.

You will hear the scripture in Malachi more often and most times with the robbing and cursing parts emphasized over everything else. But this is not God. God does not guilt us into giving. He does not try to persuade us to give with repetitious pleas. He does not use the word as a tool to condemn us. As a matter of fact, He wants us to give freely and with joy according to 2 Corinthians 9:7-8, which again says, *"So let each one give <u>as he purposes in his heart</u>, not grudgingly* *or of necessity; for God loves a cheerful giver. And God is able to make all grace abound toward you, that you, always having all sufficiency in all things, may have an abundance for every good work."* And this is the part where there is a lack of faith… believing that GOD, not the people, will provide abundance for every good work.

When preachers berate the congregation into giving, they are operating in faithlessness and weaponizing the Word of God to compel people to give instead of trusting God to place "purpose" in the heart of the believer to give, and do not believe God will fulfil His promise to cause grace, sufficiency, and abundance to abound toward them and the church "for every good work."

When the scripture says, "not grudgingly or of necessity", that translates to "not with grief or sorrow out of compulsion or pressure." In other words, we should not be giving because we feel guilty, we should not be giving with an attitude of regret and reluctance. We should not be giving because the preacher said so. We should not be giving because a prophet told us we must sow into a word as if we're paying a fortune teller. Instead, we should be giving with joy by faith, that we may be blessed! When our giving becomes a faithless, fearful, guilt-filled, obligatory act, we void the blessing and reward that comes with giving.

Our blessings and financial well-being have never been, and never will be, tied to a tithe. Anyone who preaches differently is not speaking with understanding or by inspiration from the Spirit of the Living God. I say this with confidence, not only from personal experience, but common sense.

If wealth and financial increase were a direct result of tithing, why are there so many wealthy, wicked people in the world? If giving a tenth of your income was the key that unlocked the door to financial freedom in your life, then why aren't all the atheists, agnostics, Hindus, Buddhists, Muslims, and everyone in between poor and destitute? How do we account for the millionaires and billionaires of this world who completely deny the existence of God and live a life entirely unaccountable to anyone but themselves? These facts cannot be reconciled; therefore, the "prosperity gospel" theory cannot be sustained, it's simply false. Just one more tool the enemy has used to manipulate us into the bondage of self-righteousness, and in doing so, kept us from receiving the gift of Salvation in its entirety.

If we need more evidence to put this false doctrine to rest, all we have to do is look at the ministry of Jesus Christ. Not once did he raise an offering. Not once did he request an offering before or after healing someone. Not once did he require the crowds that flocked to him to give him money.

Preachers are quick to teach that we should live as Christ lived, but how often do you hear preachers teaching that we should give as Christ gave? Not often, and perhaps it's because there isn't a single biblical account of Jesus giving or collecting tithes during His ministry. What you will find is that he taught the people, he inspired the people, he encouraged the people, and he healed the people, and as a result of the great gift they had received, they were compelled by their faith and their own testimony, to bring offerings to the body out of their substance, for the work of the ministry... they gave with a willing heart, by faith, not to obtain something, but because of what they had already obtained.

CHAPTER 3

giving is worship

"With integrity, you have nothing to fear, since you have nothing to hide. With integrity, you will do the right thing, so you will have no guilt." -Zig Ziglar

Now that we know the biblical origin of tithing and having dispelled the myth and tainted doctrine of the "prosperity gospel", let us understand fully the purpose for giving, so that it may find its place in our hearts. We are called to live a life of integrity, and this includes our giving. We cannot afford to give under the oppression of guilt and condemnation, as if Christ had not died for our sins. We cannot afford to give from a position of pressure, as if God were holding our blessings hostage. We cannot afford to give under the ruse of rules, rituals, and regulations, as if we could ever attain the righteousness of the law. We cannot afford to give under the expectation of exchange, as if we could ever afford to purchase with money anything God has paid in full to provide with the blood bought sacrifice of His Son. The only way we can afford to give… the ONLY way we can afford to give… is as an act of worship. When we give for any other reason, we are withdrawing from an empty account, and will find ourselves giving beneath our means. I say giving "beneath our means" because giving for any other reason is a faithless act, and by doing so we not only forfeit the blessing, but subject ourselves to divine judgment.

A perfect example of giving beneath our means is found in Acts 5:1-11, here you find the story of Ananias and Sapphira, a couple who decided to give to the ministry, but did not have righteous intentions. They sold some land and brought a portion of the proceeds to the Apostles, but when they were asked if the offering was for the entire amount of the purchase price for the land, they lied. They lied because they wanted to appear to have done this great act, they wanted people to think they were giving so much to the ministry, but their giving was not an act of worship, it was an act of pride and a futile attempt to either curry favor with the Apostles, or at minimum establish themselves as somehow superior to others through their giving. The amount of the offering wasn't as important as the intent of the offering. Their offering was void of integrity, which not only rendered it worthless, but according to Acts 5:3-6, cost them more than they could afford –

> *3 But Peter said, "Ananias, why has Satan filled your heart to lie to the Holy Spirit and keep back part of the price of the land for yourself? 4 While it remained, was it not your own? And after it was sold, was it not in your own control? Why have you conceived this thing in your heart? You have not lied to men but to God."*
>
> *5 Then Ananias, hearing these words, fell down and breathed his last. So great fear came upon all those who heard these things. 6 And the young men arose and wrapped him up, carried him out, and buried him.*

You see here that Peter says Ananias literally lied to the Holy Spirit by bringing a deceitful offering. And furthermore, he clearly states the offering was completely his to give, he had no obligation to give any of it, let alone all of it. But stating that he was giving all of it, when he actually wasn't, was a lie he told to God, not to the Apostles, and not to the church.

If you keep reading you will see that his wife Sapphira had the same opportunity to tell the truth, but she chose to lie, and like her husband before her, God snatched the breath out of her body and she died on the spot, and was then carried out and buried beside her husband. Two lives lost, over a deceitful offering.

This makes it crystal clear that God is not concerned with the money, He is concerned with the motive. Each one of us are individually accountable to worship with a pure heart, and our giving should come from a pure place. We should not be bullied, pressured, coerced, intimidated or otherwise compelled to give from any other place than a heart of worship. Giving from any other source will spiritually bankrupt us and cause us to be cursed by something God intended to be a blessing.

Just as we should not give beneath our means, we also cannot afford to give above our means. You may be saying, now hold on, exactly how can we give above our means? When we give just because the law says we should tithe, when we use Malachi 3:8 as our foundation, when we choose to ignore the life and sacrifice of Christ, when we allow ourselves to be guilted into giving, when we give as an act of performance instead of worship, we are giving above our means. If we are not careful, we may even attempt to establish a counterfeit standard of righteousness through our giving. And in doing so, we glorify ourselves instead of God.

We have to be very careful that our giving does not become a show, a performance for the pastor or others to see how much we are able to contribute to the ministry. It can be so easy to give with a self-righteous attitude, just as the Pharisee in Luke 18:9-14 apparently did –

9 Then Jesus told this story to some who had great confidence in their own righteousness and scorned everyone else: 10 "Two men went to the Temple to pray. One was a Pharisee, and the other was a despised tax collector. 11 The Pharisee stood by himself and prayed this prayer: 'I thank you, God, that I am not like other people—cheaters, sinners, adulterers. I'm certainly not like that tax collector! 12 I fast twice a week, and I give you a tenth of my income.'

13 "But the tax collector stood at a distance and dared not even lift his eyes to heaven as he prayed. Instead, he beat his chest in sorrow, saying, 'O God, be merciful to me, for I am a sinner.' 14 I tell you, this sinner, not the Pharisee, returned home justified before God. For those who exalt themselves will be humbled, and those who humble themselves will be exalted."

The scriptures explain how he made sure to point out how he was not like other men, like the extortioners, unjust, and adulterers, and like the tax collector that was praying beside him. He stated in his prayer that he fasted twice a week and that he gave a tithe of all his possessions. But then the Bible speaks of the tax collector, how he was so humble that he would not even raise his eyes to heaven, but acknowledged his faults and asked God to be merciful to him. The scriptures go on to say that this man was justified, and the Pharisee was not.

This man was obviously not a student of the law, he might have been involved in some shady dealings, we don't know the details; but what we do know is that he knew he was nothing compared to God and he had God to thank for everything he had. On the other hand, the Pharisee believed he was better than this man, simply because he kept the law and paid his tithes. This is as much a failure of the church in that day as it was a character flaw. The Pharisee had been conditioned by the culture of the church to believe that he had somehow elevated himself to a standard of righteousness the gentleman beside him either would not, or could not attain. Not only that, but he made his prayer to God a conversation of comparison, instead of a heart talk with His creator. He wasn't talking to God, because God has no need for us to remind Him of how holy we think we are, instead he was making himself feel better about himself, by comparing himself with others, and the Bible clearly instructs us not to engage in fruitless comparisons (Galatians 6:4-5). Somewhere along the way, the Pharisee learned to practice prayer in this manner, most likely from those who trained him, prestigious scholars of the law and influential Jewish leaders who cultivated a culture of superiority and exemplified a self-righteous disposition toward others. Unfortunately, this issue remains a thorn in the Body of Christ even today.

Have you ever noticed that in some churches, the ones who give more are treated differently by the leadership? They have access to the pastor that others don't, they have the pastor's ear, and they are usually allowed into the inner circle of the ministry, even if they have nothing to contribute other than their presence and pocketbooks. They are essentially leasing a status in the church, and expect to receive preferential treatment because of what they contribute financially.

Like the Pharisee, they have convinced themselves of their worth, and unfortunately, leaders often do little to disabuse them of this grandiose perception of themselves, but instead perpetuate their sense of superiority by placating to their demands due to fear of losing the financial support. They may not say it, but they believe they have bought their righteousness with their tithe, they love to boast about themselves, they relish in recognition, and they always feel like they're doing the church a favor... and they don't mind occasionally reminding the pastor of this when it suits them.

Jesus had strong words for people with this haughty disposition, He addresses the matter in Matthew 23:23, where he says, *"Woe to you, scribes and Pharisees, hypocrites! For you pay tithe of mint and anise and cumin, and have neglected the weightier matters of the law: justice and mercy and faith. These you ought to have done, without leaving the others undone. Blind guides, who strain out a gnat and swallow a camel!"* In this scripture Jesus was neither condemning them for tithing, nor celebrating the fact that they do; but He was pointing out how religious they had become in adhering to the law yet failed to develop a relationship with the God they claim to serve. In the scriptures following this verse, Jesus continues to point out how they perform outwardly for men to see, but inwardly they are hypocrites.

Many preachers will actually try to use this same passage of scripture to justify teaching tithing as a mandatory obligation of the believer; claiming this is evidence in the New Testament that we are obligated to tithe; once again, this is a false doctrine and misrepresentation of scripture.

We have to not only look at what Jesus was saying, but who he was talking to. He was talking to the scribes and Pharisees, he was talking to the Jews. He was not talking to the gentiles, which is what we are. Some will say this applies because we have been grafted into the Body of Christ (Ephesians 2:11-19, Romans 11:13-24), and while we have indeed been grafted in, and adopted as sons, we were not grafted into the law, we were grafted into this royal priesthood through grace, we were adopted into the Body of Faith by the blood of Jesus, which is apparent in Ephesians 2:13-18 –

13 But now in Christ Jesus you who once were far off have been brought near by the blood of Christ. 14 For He Himself is our peace, who has made both one, and has broken down the middle wall of separation, 15 having abolished in His flesh the enmity, that is, the law of commandments contained in ordinances, so as to create in Himself one new man from the two, thus making peace, 16 and that He might reconcile them both to God in one body through the cross, thereby putting to death the enmity. 17 And He came and preached peace to you who were afar off and to those who were near. 18 For through Him we both have access by one Spirit to the Father.

Look closely at the love of God illuminated here for us, how God, in the form of His Son Jesus Christ, combined the sinful nature of the flesh with the righteousness of the law into one Man, Jesus Christ, put the battle between them to death on the cross, and thereby reconciled us to the Father. Knowing this, understanding that the Prince of Peace has made peace between us and the law, why then would we cherry pick the law of tithing and choose to nullify this sacrifice? Why isn't the blood of Jesus enough? If we believe that we are blessed if we tithe, and cursed if we don't, then can we really say we believe that Jesus Saves... to the utmost, Jesus Saves? No, we cannot say it, and we do not believe it, because if we did, no one could convince us to substitute the grace of God with the law. If we truly believed what Jesus did was enough, then we would humble ourselves to the fact that if we cannot keep one law, we cannot keep any, and to live by the law, is to die by the law. This is a standard we cannot afford to live by, which is exactly why Jesus Paid It All.

When we give, it should be an act of worship, with a posture of humility, not for performance, knowing there is no amount we could ever afford to pay in order to make ourselves righteous. There are no blessings we can purchase, and no curses we can protect ourselves from with our pocketbooks and bank accounts. We serve a Good, Good Father, whose desire it is to give us every good gift. This love and this amazing grace cannot be bought, or leased for a tithe, it can only be received, and returned in gratitude to God, as an act of worship.

CHAPTER 4

not by sight

"Faith talks in the language of God. Doubt talks in the language of man." -E.W. Kenyon

We like to think that we are doing a great and wonderful thing by giving a tithe, but the truth of the matter is, it all belongs to God. And if you give $50 out of $500 when God told you to give $300, you give $300 but you hated to do it, or you look down on others who cannot give as much, you might as well have kept the money because the blessing is cancelled.

There is absolutely nothing wrong with tithing, as long as you're aware that it is not a requirement. As long as you are not being manipulated or made to feel guilty because you don't do it. As long as you are not doing it resentfully, out of regret or with compulsion. And as long as you don't allow tithing to limit you and what God has for you.

We can limit ourselves and God by thinking that if we give 10% we have contributed what is required and don't need to go any further. The truth is we should just be obedient to what God asks us to give regardless of how much it is, and many times it's not 10%. It may be more, it may be less, and sometimes it may be a sacrifice.

Whatever the amount, it will be God, through the Holy Spirit, who should prompt you to do so out of faith, not because you've sat through the third round of a re-run offering and are ready to go home.

God may sometimes ask us to give what we think we don't have, give from money we have saved up to do something else with, or bless a family or person with a financial gift or material item we've purchased for ourselves. When God asks us to do this, we must do our best to be obedient, because He is never trying to take anything from us by asking us to give, instead He wants to get something to us through our giving.

A clear example of this is found in 1 Kings Chapter 17, which gives the account of the prophet Elijah being sent by God to the city of Zarephath, where God commanded a widow there to feed him. He arrived in Zarephath and as God said there was a widow there, but when he asked her for some bread, she told him there wasn't enough for him, only enough to make a small meal for herself and her son and then they would die. Elijah instructed her to make him a small cake first and then make hers. She obeyed his instructions, and because of her obedience the Bible says her bin of flour was not used up and her oil did not run dry.

What if she doubted God? What if she believed that what she could see, what was tangible, was all that she had? What if she thought Elijah's request was unreasonable given her circumstances? We can assume she would have done what she said she was going to do, fix something for her and her son and then die.

We have to do our very best to move quickly when God is telling us to sacrifice financially... when GOD is telling us. Because if we wait, if we hesitate, we may allow the enemy to put doubt into our minds about what God asked us to do. We may begin to think of all we need to do with the money. We may begin to think of how little we have or what we intended to do, and all the while we are missing our opportunity to be a blessing and to be blessed.

Not all of us are struggling financially. Some of us are doing very well; we are living comfortably, we have everything we need and most of the things we want, so the idea of giving 10% doesn't bother us at all. The idea of giving 20% or even 30% has no effect on us either, so we are quick to give at offering time without a second thought.

Does our ability to give 10% mean that we are being obedient to God? Does our ability to give a greater offering than most others place us on another level of blessing or favor from God? Does our ability to step in and give those types of offerings that the pastor or preacher is pleading for in their hour of faithlessness or ignorance earn us any points with God? No, and we can see that in Luke 21:1-4, which states,

> *1 As Jesus looked up, he saw the rich putting their gifts into the temple treasury. 2 He also saw a poor widow put in two very small copper coins. 3 "Truly I tell you," he said, "this poor widow has put in more than all the others. 4 All these people gave their gifts out of their wealth; but she out of her poverty put in all she had to live on."*

Now this is yet another facet of giving – giving out of your own need, as an act of faith, not under pressure, but as a matter of purpose settled within your heart. This woman was a widow, she was in an impoverished state, and she gave two mites. A mite is the smallest copper coin used in Palestine, and it is worth approximately 1/8 of a cent. And yet Jesus says she gave more than everyone else. Why? Not because it was greater monetarily. Not because she wanted to be seen or recognized. Actually, I can imagine it might have been quite the opposite. She may have felt like what she gave didn't matter compared to what everyone else was giving. She may have even struggled to give the two mites for fear that others would see that she was giving so little. But God says she gave more than everyone.

What she gave would be the equivalent to everyone else giving up everything they had, because that is what she did. It's not likely that those who had more than enough would have been so generous. In fact, it says in Matthew 19:24 that it's easier for a camel to go through the eye of a needle than for a rich man to enter the kingdom of God. This may seem like an exaggeration, but if you just look at the world around you it is apparent Jesus was speaking the truth. There is absolutely nothing wrong with being wealthy, in fact God wants us all to live comfortably. However, it is so difficult for people who have wealth to depend on God or look to God because they somehow believe that they have everything they need; even though we are presented daily with evidence that money is not enough to make anyone happy or give anyone peace.

Just in the last year, people have taken their own lives or the lives of others because they were faced with a situation they didn't know how to handle. They built their whole lives around their social status and their wealth, and when those things were threatened, they found themselves in a state of hopelessness.

It's not enough to have money or even give a lot of money because you have it to give. If you give $5,000 to a ministry, that ministry may be very grateful and see that as an amazing gift. But if you are a millionaire you won't even miss it, it was nothing, there was no sacrifice, there was no consideration at all concerning what God wanted you to give, you may have given just because you had it to give. Have you ever considered that may not have been good ground to sow into?

Have you ever considered that God may not have wanted you to give to that person or ministry, or that God may have wanted you to give more or less? Or did you let pride dictate your giving, the desire to be recognized by men, wanting to save the day with your checkbook, or wanting to create an artificial relationship with God and the church through your finances?

We need a real relationship with God. And we need direction from the Holy Spirit in all things. I was once told that every good thing is not a God thing. We must seek God concerning our giving, be in position to listen, and be willing to obey when God speaks. It all belongs to God, so the best we can do is give *from* God, not give *to* God.

We really like to think that we're doing God or the church a favor by giving. Here's some news, God doesn't need your money! That's right, He doesn't need your money to do anything He has decided to do in this earth. And God most certainly Does NOT want your Bill Money! It is God Himself who has given you provision to pay your bills. What God needs is your obedience. He needs your willingness. He needs your availability. And He needs access to everything you are and everything you have, which is all He made you and all He gave you.

CHAPTER 5

giving from vs. giving to

" I have found that among its other benefits, giving liberates the soul of the giver." -Maya Angelou

Sometimes God will tell us to give to a ministry or person that we don't think is deserving, but we aren't the judge of who is deserving and who isn't. And sometimes God won't let us give to a cause that we feel like emptying our bank account for. We have to understand that God knows more than we could ever know, and that there is a valid reason for everything He asks us to do.

When we are giving from God versus giving to God, it eliminates the pride factor, the poverty factor, the pastor or preacher factor, and our giving becomes an act of worship, simply because God is worthy.

When we begin to give to God from a perspective of worship, then we stop giving because we want something from God, we stop trying to bribe God for blessings, we stop gambling with our bill money, we stop giving to be seen and recognized, we stop trying to pay for healing, we stop trying to pay for a breakthrough, we stop trying to pay for the anointing, we stop being manipulated into paying taxes on our salvation, we stop believing the false doctrine that states those of us who have received the Lord Jesus Christ as Savior are cursed because we don't tithe.

There is a blessing that comes from giving. Not just money but giving what God asks us to give. Our time, our talent, our gifts, our love, our faithfulness, our resources. We don't want to miss out on our blessing by limiting ourselves and God to 10% of our income. Why not just be obedient and put yourself in position for limitless abundance? We must be careful not to get caught up in religious giving, habitual acts of empty routine. Becoming like those Jesus spoke of in Matthew 15:8-9 when He stated, *"These people draw near to Me with their mouth, and honor Me with their lips, but their heart is far from Me, teaching as doctrines the commandments of men."*

I'd like to take a moment to share a personal testimony. I was attending a church called Rainbow

Christian Center about 12 years ago. The church was preparing to expand by leasing out an additional portion of the complex where they were holding services. About the time the announcement was made I was a few weeks out from receiving my annual bonus. God spoke to me during service plain and clear, and instructed me to pay the first month's lease on the new portion of the building. My bonus was a little over $1,400, and the lease was about $830 if I remember correctly. That means God asked me to give not 10%, but nearly 60% of my bonus as an offering. Now, I had to pray on this because you know I already had plans for that money! BUT, my spirit would not be at peace with keeping it, I had to obey the voice of God.

Soon as my bonus came, I took out the money and gave it to my pastors at the time, Pastors Larry and Delores Brown. This was a major faith move for me, I don't think I'd ever given this much in an offering before. But God honored my obedience, and shortly after that I was promoted at work. Now, do I believe I bought a blessing? No, there's nothing God can give me that I could afford to buy. But I do believe God honored my obedience, and I believe this is a perfect example of Matthew 6:33, *"But seek first the kingdom of God and His righteousness, and all these things shall be added to you."*

I did not give 60% of my bonus because my pastors asked me to, I gave it because God told me to. And had I given 10%, that would've fulfilled the law, but would've actually been disobedience on my part, because I heard God clearly instruct me to give more. The bottom line is, ask God what He would have you to do, and when He speaks don't hesitate; and He will not hesitate to bless you. If you are new in Christ and don't quite know when you are hearing from God over the noise of tradition and religion, then give what you feel lead to give in your heart. It doesn't matter if it's 10% or $10, the point is, start somewhere and be faithful! And as you grow in the grace of God, your faith will grow, and that faith will extend to your offerings. Eventually, you will find it easier to give, and as you exercise your ear, the more clearly you will hear God speak to your heart.

If you don't have money to give, you should give when and where you can. There are many ways you can advance the vision of the ministry without money. I've had members of my congregation cut the grass at the church for no charge. Members will come and clean the bathrooms, kitchen, and sanctuary. Members will go visit the nursing homes and serve at the soup kitchens. I've had members bring food or groceries for one of our outreach events that they bought with their EBT cards. They didn't have money to give, but they brought what they could, and I promise you, they are not any less blessed, their offering is recognized and rewarded by God. It is God who qualifies and quantifies our offerings! It has very little to do with the amount, and everything to do with the heart.

Do not allow the enemy to condemn you if you miss an opportunity to give or something comes up and you don't have it to give. It is God who has blessed us with the ability to pay our bills and take care of our families, and we should be good stewards of our finances as instructed in Scripture and take care of our own homes.

It is not an act of faith to give the church your light bill money then pray to the same God who gave you the job that allowed you to earn the money for your light bill, to give it to you again; and yet, even I, in my ignorance, have done this in my past more than once. It is not God who makes us feel guilty about giving, He does not condemn His children. However, we may feel a strong conviction or urging from God to give, and when it is from God, and God alone, we should obey and open up our hand to Him; not because we are expecting something back, but because we know it is already His, and it is we who are giving back. We can stand on the promises of God, knowing that we are blessed, knowing that if we seek Him first we will have everything we need, knowing that He will not place more on us than we are able to bear, knowing that if He is asking, He is also standing by ready to give, and that we can never out-give God.

If you are being spiritually fed by your pastor, empowered and encouraged by fellowship, and you are growing in your walk with God, make sure you are giving faithfully to that place of worship so that the ministry that is blessing you can continue to bless others. If the lights and water are on it's because it takes money to pay the utilities. If your children are attending children's church it's because someone is paying for the staff, ministry materials, and snacks that help give them a meaningful worship experience. If your church is actively serving the community by operating food banks, sheltering the homeless, ministering in prisons, or offering mentoring programs to the youth, it's because the finances are available to do so.

Everything that you enjoy about your worship experience has a financial element to it, and if you are benefiting from that, I believe God will touch your heart with a purpose to give, and the Holy Spirit will prompt you to contribute toward its maintenance. It really is that simple.

Let us be like the church described in Acts 4:32, where the scriptures state *"the multitude of those who believed were of one heart and one soul; neither did anyone say that any of the things he possessed was his own, but they had all things in common. And with great power the apostles gave witness to the resurrection of the Lord Jesus. And great grace was upon them all. Nor was there anyone among them who lacked; for all who were possessors of lands or houses sold them, and brought the proceeds of the things that were sold, and laid them at the apostles' feet; and they distributed to each as anyone had need."*

Now, I am not telling anyone to go sell anything and bring the money to the church. What I am saying is your giving should be based upon your love for God and what God is leading you to do. And as a member of your local assembly, you should want to see Kingdom works go forward. And having one heart with God, being assigned to the shepherd and aligned with the vision of that ministry, give as the Spirit leads you, and you will obtain favor, your needs will be met, and so will the needs of your brothers and sisters.

I pray this book has helped you to better understand how and why God wants us to give. It is my prayer that everyone who reads this book will release themselves from the burden of guilt and condemnation, and receive the favor and blessing of giving, according to Luke 6:38, *"Give, and it will be given to you: good measure, pressed down, shaken together, and running over."*

If this book was a blessing to you, please sow a copy into someone's life so they can understand the freedom of giving, and receive the blessing of giving, as an expression of faith, and an act of worship.

reflection & discussion

"Faith talks in the language of God. Doubt talks in the language of man." -E.W. Kenyon

The following questions can be used for self-reflection and to encourage conversation in group discussions concerning the topic of Godly Giving.

1. Did this book help you to better understand what God is requiring from you financially as a believer?

2. What have you been taught about tithing?

3. Have you personally read what the Scriptures say about tithing before reading this book?

4. Do you feel guilty when you don't tithe?

5. Do you believe that you are cursed when you don't tithe? Blessed when you do? Why or why not?

6. Have you ever struggled with the decision of tithing vs. making a purchase or paying a bill?

7. What did you decide to do and why?

8. Do you agree that finances are essential to effective ministry?

9. Are you willing to consistently contribute to the

maintenance of your church and to the kingdom initiatives of your local assembly?

10. If you don't attend a church locally, but regularly watch a certain minister or ministry online, would you consider giving to them regularly?

11. We have read in the Scriptures where God has asked for more than money, what can you do to be a blessing to your church or your community besides giving money?

Scriptural References

Following is a list of Bible verses in the Old and New Testament related to tithing and Spirit-led giving for personal study.

Genesis 14:20 – Melchizedek comes out to meet Abraham, as Abraham gives him a tithe of the spoils of his victory.

Genesis 28:20-22 – After the vision of God's renewed covenant, Jacob initiates a covenant with God vowing to give him a tithe of what he receives from the promised land.

Leviticus 27:30-32 – The specifications of the tithe is introduced into the Law of Moses.

Numbers 18:21 – The tithe is dedicated to the Levites for their inheritance for their devoted work in the tabernacle.

Deuteronomy 14:22-29 – God gives instructions on how to disperse and exchange the tithe.

Deuteronomy 16:10 – An Old Testament ceremony paralleled the future Church with a freewill offering.

Malachi 3:8-10 – God reprimands the Priests for delivering up lame and blemished offerings, and by their actions caused the people not to take their offerings seriously.

Matthew 6:33 – But seek first the kingdom of God and His righteousness, and all these things shall be added to you.

Matthew 23:23 – Jesus rebukes the Pharisees for not obeying the weightier matters of the law along with tithing.

Luke 6:38 – Give, and it will be given to you. A good measure, pressed down, shaken together and running over, will be poured into your lap. For with the measure you use, it will be measured to you.

Luke 11:42 – A parallel passage of Matthew 23:23 as Jesus rebukes the Pharisees for not obeying the weightier matters of the law along with tithing.

Luke 18:12 – A Pharisee brags about his obedience to the law and tithing.

John 7:21-24 – The church is not commanded to follow the ordinances of Abraham and Moses.

Romans 8:32 – Giving tithes and offerings in exchange for blessings is not an eternal principle nor character trait of God.

Romans 12:8; Galatians 5:18-25 – We are now lead and instructed by The Holy Spirit, not the Mosaic law.

2 Corinthians 8:12 – "For if the willingness is there, the gift is acceptable according to what one has, not according to what one does not have."

2 Corinthians 9:7 – "Each of you should give what you have decided in your heart to give, not reluctantly or under compulsion, for God loves a cheerful giver."

2 Corinthians 9:8-9 – "And God is able to bless you abundantly, so that in all things at all times, having all that you need, you will abound in every good work. As it is written: "He has dispersed abroad, He has given to the poor; His righteousness endures forever."

2 Corinthians 9:10 – "Now he who supplies seed to the sower and bread for food will also supply and increase your store of seed and will enlarge the harvest of your righteousness."

2 Corinthians 9:11 – "You will be enriched in every way so that you can be generous on every occasion, and through us your generosity will result in thanksgiving to God."

Genesis to Revelation – There is no commandment from God to the born again, neither is there a Scriptural foundation, obligation, or requirement for the New Testament Church to tithe.

A Note from the Author

I would love to hear your opinion about this book and the topic of Tithes and Offerings. I welcome your constructive feedback and testimony of how this book has affected your life.

Please send comments and questions to desimberrose@gmail.com.

The Truth Series is a publication offered by Desimber Rose Wattleton for personal growth and development. If you would like to make a donation to this ministry, please send your gift to the following address:

>   Attn: The Truth Series
>   P.O. Box 1075
>   Taylors, SC 29687
>   Cash App $AskTheWord
>   PayPal: desimberrose@gmail.com

If you would like to book Pastor Desimber Rose for a speaking engagement at your business, church, seminar or conference, please call 864-999-8237 or email desimberrose@gmail.com.

Made in the USA
Columbia, SC
16 July 2022